WATER TANKS OF CHICAGO

WATER TANKS OF CHICAGO
A VANISHING URBAN LEGACY

PHOTOGRAPHS & PAINTINGS
BY LARRY W. GREEN

Larry W. Green

Wicker Park Press, Ltd.

WATER TANKS OF CHICAGO:
A VANISHING URBAN LEGACY

PHOTOGRAPHS & PAINTINGS
BY LARRY W. GREEN

Published in 2007 by
Wicker Park Press, Ltd.
P.O. Box 5318
River Forest, Illinois 60305-5318
www.wickerparkpress.com

Library of Congress Cataloging-in-Publication Data on file with the publisher.

ISBN 13: 978-0-9789676-0-4
ISBN 10: 0-9789676-0-7

For Nathan and Elizabeth.

Grateful acknowledgements to

Merritt Franco

Mel Theobald

Eric Miller

Greg Lackncr

Steve Garnett

and my loving wife Janet.

Thanks so much for helping me and
guiding me through this process.

FOREWORD

LARRY GREEN'S CHICAGO WATERTANK SERIES

Many places have water-tanks; they've been fixtures of the urban landscape
in most American cities and towns. But Larry Green's water-tanks belong to
Chicago. They aren't New York's, they are ours, symbolic of this place, this
city. Perhaps that's why a visitor to an exhibition of Green's work, a man
who'd never bought a work of art in his life, bought one of the water-tank
series – wherever he took the painting, Chicago was with him – he 'knew'
the subject, he 'knew' it was Chicago, and the artwork 'grounded' him in
place and time. So while the subjects of Green's paintings are not unique to
Chicago, they speak powerfully of this place – these are paintings that are
not only specific narratives, they are also about iconic objects of the past,
and recent or present history.

Is there an element of nostalgia in this? In some ways there is, for city
ordinances now require that many of these old, creaking, rusty and usually
redundant structures need to be removed – they'll all be gone in a few years.
But Green isn't painting them for nostalgia, he's an artist who is fascinated
by how indeed they are all the same – but every one is different – how they
peek up atop old buildings, how you see them out of the corner of your eye,
down alleys and above the nice clean façades, anonymous but with a crisp
graphic presence. The series grew from casual sketches that were small in
scale – an artist's notes taken while looking at the streetscape – but have
grown to be paintings on a serious and well-considered scale. He likes the
sculptural form of the water-tanks, how they are strongly backlit and stand in
stark colorless contrast with skies and the building-scape. And Green has
removed nearly all the narrative color in these works, reducing the palette to
an almost monochromatic range, making the scumble and brushwork create
the contrasts. He makes carefully-constructed formal compositions, anchored
by the powerful silhouettes and forms of the tanks, centre-stage, flanked by
curtain walls, fences, wires, poles that serve to frame the towers. Painters
like Charles Scheeler, and the German photographers Bernd and Hilla
Becher, have imbued ordinary industrial structures like these tanks, grain-silos
and coalmine winding-gear with such graphic power that we see these
easily-dismissed pieces of engineering as though they were quite new.

So Chicago's crumbling water-tanks take on a new significance when seen in Green's paintings – surely we knew they were there, they'd registered, but they weren't the star of the street-show. But we've woken up to them, become part of his celebration of them as dynamic incidents in what is clearly a Chicago landscape. We see them like the man who bought the painting because he 'knew' the place where these tanks existed, they move from being just industrial detritus to emblems in our perception of what bits-and-pieces go to make up the real, or remembered, Chicago.

Anthony Jones
President
School of the Art Institute of Chicago

EDITOR'S NOTE

CHICAGO TANK CITY

The water tanks that dot the urban terrain of commercial and factory buildings in Chicago hark back to a different time and place. A water tank is a highly efficient system for keeping water on hand as a precious resource, and while it has been replaced by modern sprinkler systems and computerized technology, there is nothing about a water tank that you can improve upon for its sheer practicality. It's a shame they have not continued to be utilized for their original intentions, and they are rapidly going the way of such Chicago dinosaurs as Meigs Field, the Stock Exchange Building, Polk Brothers Department Store, the Granada Theater and Pilgrim Baptist Church.

Water tanks remind me of telephone poles and telegraph wires that were strung across the landscape for the practical purposes of basic communication. They were built for much the same reason the railroads tore through the American wilderness in the 19th century and meant progress, increased commerce and the free movement of ideas. Now we have wireless communication, cars, airplanes and the Internet. Who is to say that telephone poles will not be chopped down in years to come, and replaced by a newer mode of delivery? Like the water tanks of Chicago, telephone poles and exposed wires in this book are a symbol of another era, and there are poignant examples of the juxtaposition of wires and water tanks with their majestic steel platforms. They convey a grand beauty and a stark expediency. Wires carry electricity and sound, water tanks store vast amounts of water for later use: a no-nonsense approach to conquering nature.

There has been a recent effort among preservationists and architectural enthusiasts to save the water tanks of Chicago. The photographs and paintings of Larry Green are simple and powerful and convey a blast-furnace realism. It is all about keen observation of things in your environment, and this book is a kind of clarion call to save the magnificent and thoroughly distinctive water tanks in Chicago, and to make readers aware of something in their midst which is at once commonplace and yet extraordinary. The water tanks incorporate everything that is iconic about the city of Chicago, and this book is an attempt to make you see it for yourself.

Chicago created itself over time and rose like a smoldering phoenix from the ashes of the Great Fire of 1871. This catastrophe, steeped as it is in myth and legend, was supposed to be the end of time for the great metropolis by the lake. Chicago proved itself otherwise in the years that ensued, and its rebirth culminated with Chicago hosting the World's Columbian Exposition in 1893. In twenty-two short years since the devastation of the fire, Chicago had refashioned itself into a world showcase city on par with the grand European capitols of Paris, Vienna and London.

Out of the wild urban jungle rose the rooftop water tanks, defining the skyline with their cast iron bases welded in place for eternity, and making their own bold statement. Chicago inoculated itself against another disaster by storing water in its very midst, and the tanks themselves speak powerfully to the history and development of the city itself and cry out to be saved for future generations. The water tanks were key players in the ongoing transformation of the landscape into the international city we know today, and it is high time they were recognized for their important contribution and given proper landmark status by the authorities. Here is a glimpse of the state of the water tanks in the early 21st century, and hopefully this book will open people's eyes to the beauty and value of Chicago's water tanks.

Eric Lincoln Miller
Editor & Publisher
Wicker Park Press, Ltd.

PHOTOGRAPHS

These are Chicago's water tanks.

They are popularly known as water towers, but actually they are water tanks, and you will find them dotted throughout the municipal landscape.

They are a fascinating part of Chicago history
and one of the city's unique architectural symbols.

They are a monument to the position the
city occupies on the architectural map.

You see them overlooking, with silent observation, everyday life in the metropolis.

They have been scattered throughout the city
since the 19th century.

The water tanks were originally used as a water reserve, created in response to vital concerns over firefighting capabilities after the grim lessons of the Great Chicago Fire in 1871.

Over 1,300 of them were constructed as a water supplement system to help ensure a similar disaster would not strike again.

They have not yet gone the way
of the dinosaurs, but they are
nearing the point of extinction.

Due to modern technology in fire fighting, water supply improvements and the archaic and crumbling structures of buildings outliving their prime, the water tanks have rapidly been disappearing.

This is a shame, since they are striking landmarks that at once define the Chicago skyline.

The water tanks are as much a signature of what Chicago was and is as Lake Michigan, State Street, and the Gold Coast.

Most Chicago residents and visitors take them for
granted and seldom realize they are even there,
until gently reminded of their existence.

But, that time of existence is running out.

As I ride the Chicago Transit Authority elevated trains, I see them occasionally spotted across the skyline in between factory buildings, atop apartment buildings, and in almost every neighborhood.

Every year I see less and less
of the great water tanks.

Vacant platforms with ghost tanks stand where some had been.

They are victims of age and time.

Marked by old and rotting wood,
rusting iron and steel, the rodent and insect-
laden structures have been vanishing.

There are a few water tanks in particular that
I had grown comfortable with seeing every day.

But, as the Near North, Westside and South Loop neighborhoods have begun to redevelop and gentrify, more and more of them have disappeared.

Where water tanks used to tower above buildings in the city, I now find the towers empty with whatever survived being used for glorified billboards or telecommunication platforms.

Whenever I am away from the city, the water tanks are among the things I miss the most.

There was once a gentleman, years ago,
who bought a few of my water tank paintings.

He had moved to Seattle and he told me the images of the great water tanks were a fond reminder of Chicago for him.

He simply did not want to forget them.

Whenever I get the chance, and I have my camera with me,
I will photograph the remaining great water tanks that reveal
themselves to me as I travel through the city.

I do not think there will be a time when I will not seek out the water tanks.

Once you are aware of their existence,
you realize how majestic and deeply reflective
they are of Chicago and its intriguing history.

You begin to see them as you have never looked at them before.

PAINTINGS

Urban Landscape, 2006
36" x 60"
Acrylic on canvas

Dark Tower, 2006
40" x 30"
Acrylic on canvas

Water Tank in Black & White, 2007
24" x 36"
Acrylic on canvas

Water Tank Silhouette, 2006
36" x 60"
Acrylic on canvas

Wicker Park Tower, 2006
30" x 40"
Acrylic on canvas

Urban Twilight, 2006
24" x 30"
Acrylic on canvas

Urban Sunset, 2006
24" x 30"
Acrylic on canvas